allowing

happiness

on cue

I0203344

WHAT EVERYDAY PEOPLE SAY ABOUT THE PROCESS YOU'RE GOING TO LEARN IN THIS BOOK

"I would like to thank you so much for all your efforts to teach this process. It has made a big difference in my life. After all the self-help books and resources telling me to align myself, release feelings, focus on happiness, I finally have a way to do it. Now I can do all that by using your process!" ⤜ **Gigi** ⤝

"I have been having so much fun with the process, and I can't thank you enough for creating this incredible technique." ⤜ **Stephanie** ⤝

"I think you are sending out a great message and at a time when humanity really needs it. The process is simple, easy to understand and takes up very little time to do. What could be better for those of us that want things to be as easy as possible. All we have to do is use this powerful process." ⤜ **Ron** ⤝

"Marvellous! Thank you very much. I have listened to the recordings. I feel completely peaceful. I could listen to the recordings all day long. Congratulations! These words don't express it all, but they are the closest to express my admiration for your accomplishments. Heartfelt thanks and success wishes for you." ⤜ **Edna** ⤝

"I listened to the recordings last night before going to sleep. What if the process just keeps getting better and better? What if I am willing to receive love and peace in my heart?" ⤜ **Clare** ⤝

"During the process, I felt myself becoming physically lighter. I could literally feel the stress lifting off me. I've never felt such a strong reaction to any other kind of meditation or energy work." ✎ **Anita** ✎

"I happen to be very critical about the way I look. I've had my nose done, rhinoplasty (four times), liposuction, lip injections, facial line injections, and the list goes on. I've had a hard time looking at myself in pictures or on film. It's a feeling of disgust. I live in an egocentric world and it seems that if you don't look like a supermodel, you're going nowhere. When I took this feeling of disgust through the resistance exercise you teach, the next day I looked in the mirror and saw this beautiful girl looking back at me. Incredible! Honestly, you are going to put plastic surgeons out of business." ✎ **Teresa** ✎

"My husband died recently and I have had a hard time dealing with it. Going through the process gave me instant relief. I was so amazed! I felt more relaxed, my heart palpitations from stress went away, and I actually felt happier. This feeling has stayed with me. I face the future with a much clearer mind. Thanks so much!" ✎ **Jan** ✎

"I just did the cleaning audio and and giggled all the way. That is cool!" ✎ **Alain** ✎

"I must admit that while I don't understand what this process is doing for me, it is definitely doing something. My mind is so much calmer and more settled. I'm not as hard on myself. I'm forgiving myself easily and moving on from the little "mistakes" that occur in a day such as not expecting myself to be perfect and beating myself up when I'm not." ✎ **Kimberly** ✎

"Your work has been a tremendous blessing to me, and I am feeling relief from a lifetime of struggles by following your guidance."
⤳ **Grace** ⤳

"Let me tell you about my first experience with the process. My life is generally okay, and I am a happy sort of person, but certain issues come up from time to time, which bring a feeling of dread, foreboding, trepidation, and a hollow feeling in the pit of my stomach. I know that the issues are not serious and that I will get past them, but I still experience that uncomfortable, suffocating feeling so I thought I would clear this feeling with your process and it worked. It surprised me because, at the very least, I thought it might take a few sessions. I now feel lighter, as if some mental weight has been shed." ⤳ **Gita** ⤳

"I want to thank you again for your efforts and progress. I am enjoying doing the process and have taught it to several people. A friend came over from the United States and is doing it here in Israel. Connecting to the local energies too has done marvelous things for her. We worked together and did come to a state of peace longed for." ⤳ **Iris** ⤳

"Excellent technique. I had immediate results which eliminated a nagging, negative thought pattern that I was experiencing about some past regrets." ⤳ **William** ⤳

"For me, your techniques very directly came to terms with most of this gross stuff without the need to analyze the cause itself. Just break the connections permanently. Thank you so much for sharing your methods with the world." ⤳ **Peter** ⤳

"I just want to say that the process is super! It has changed my life in so many wonderful ways. I use it every day, and my family does too. My kids even use it, and I use it for them. Thank you for giving us this incredible tool!" ᔰ **April** ᔰ

"I've been listening to the download recordings now for about a month, and I didn't think anything was happening. But, when I stepped back to really look at my life, I saw many changes. I am currently in a very rigorous exercise program, walking every morning for 30 minutes and have lost about 10 pounds with hopes of many more to be released from my body. I feel much better about the spirit of who I am and that has opened up new possibilities. I am also dating a lovely man. It has been two years since anything like that has happened. I am feeling very blessed and wish to thank you for your huge contribution to these wonderful changes." ᔰ **Glo** ᔰ

"I have been practicing the process for about a year now and I do enjoy it. I have had some amazing releases. I made a "cheat sheet" and put it in a plastic sleeve so I can get to whenever I need to. Just in the last week, I have added EFT (Emotional Freedom Techniques) tapping with my cue word. Your process has amazed me from the start and together it's a real kick! Thank you very much." ᔰ **Mary** ᔰ

allowing happiness *on cue*

*A simple, powerful way to gently let
go of feelings and limiting beliefs that
block true peace of mind and happiness*

by GRANT CONNOLLY

inroads

Copyright © 2011 by Grant Connolly

All rights reserved. No part of this publication may be reproduced, stored in a retrieval system, or transmitted in any form by any means, electronic, mechanical, photocopying, recording or otherwise without prior written permission from the publisher.

The ZPoint Process is a trademark of Grant Connolly.
Inroads® is a registered trademark of Inroads, LLC.

Printed in the United States of America, United Kingdom and Australia.
Published in the United States of America by:

Inroads Publishing
P.O. Box 357
Fredericksburg, VA 22404-0357 USA

If you are unable to order this book from your local bookseller, you may be able to order directly from the publisher. Quantity discounts are available.

The music used in the download recordings was written and performed by the very talented Kevin McLeod.

Cover design by Daniel Yeager
Interior design by C. Frank Costa
Editing by Linda Miller

Library of Congress Control Number: 2011919017
ISBN: 978-0-9727671-6-3

First Edition printing 2011

Table of Contents

Disclaimer   X

Acknowledgments   XI

Dedication   XII

Foreword   XIII

What is Happiness?   1

How the Process Was Created   3

Book with Recordings   9

How to Do the ZPoint Process   13

Clearing Limiting Thoughts, Beliefs   19

Clearing Limiting Memories, Feelings   29

Healing Relationships   45

Let's Get Physical   51

More Happiness Tools   57

You Be the Change   69

Next Step... ZPoint Process Resources   77

ZPoint Process Stories   79

About the Author   101

Disclaimer

This book is provided to introduce you to a very simple, yet powerful tool called the ZPoint Process. The book represents the ideas of the author whose intention for this book is to provide information for learning about The ZPoint Process and suggest ways you might use it for self-help, personal development, and creating an all around happier life.

While the ZPoint Process quite often produces remarkable results, it is still relatively new and in the experimental stage. Given that, nothing in this book should be construed as a promise of benefits, claims of cures or a guarantee of results to be achieved.

The book is offered with the understanding that the author and publisher are not engaged in rendering medical, psychological, legal or other professional advice. The reader must take complete responsibility for his or her physical health and emotional well-being.

The information, instructions or advice presented is not intended to be a substitute for professional medical or psychological care. If you are under medical or psychological supervision, consult your healthcare professional before using any of the procedures in this book. The author and publisher disclaim any liability or loss incurred directly or indirectly as a result of the use or application of any of the contents of this book.

Acknowledgments

I'd like to thank Gary Craig for his groundbreaking creation of EFT® and Tapas Fleming for her incredible TAT® process. Both are my personal heroes—Gary for his example on how to manifest his powerful vision of helping millions of people through an ever expanding cadre of trained practitioners and Tapas for the obvious love and deep compassion she has that shines through in her TAT Process.

I thank both for their examples on how to bring the light of healing and peace to the world. Without them and the possibilities they first created, you would not be reading this book.

Finally, I'd like to acknowledge and thank Dr. Larry Nims for his creation of BSFF™ (Be Set Free Fast). His brilliant idea of using a cue word and cleaning program made the ZPoint Process possible. Thank you, Larry.

We reach for the stars by standing on the shoulders of those who come before us. Their energy, spirit and abiding intention lives on in the ZPoint Process, as you are about to discover for yourself.

Dedication

This book is dedicated to the light
that lives within all of us.

Foreword

"It is never too late to be

what you might have been."

—*T.S. ELLIOTT*

The purpose of this book and the download recordings are to help you find true and lasting peace of mind in a world filled with discord, doubt and fear. It is about letting go of those things that upset you in your personal and business relationships as well as the relationship you have with yourself. It is about finally making peace with yourself and everything and everyone in your life.

I intend to show you a simple yet profound way to change your life experience in ways that would have seemed impossible just a few short years ago. It's called The ZPoint Process and if you follow the simple steps in this book, and listen to the special downloadable recordings included, you will quickly find yourself responding to life's challenges in a far more effective, peaceful and loving way.

The book provides the basics of the ZPoint Process. It will show you everything you will need to know to release longstanding patterns of behavior that bring you no happiness or joy. You'll be guided through simple exercises to permanently release the difficult feelings that prevent you from truly enjoying your life and everything in it.

To accomplish this I'll ask you to pay attention to those *characteristic feelings* that arise as you think of certain difficult or traumatic periods of your life or bring to mind the people in your life who upset or anger you. Then, you need only listen to the *General Release* with ZPoint recording and remember to repeat a special cue word to completely release those feelings forever.

That recording, only nine minutes long, will guide you through the process to release the *characteristic feeling* that represents *all* of the uncomfortable feelings associated or connected to the person, circumstance or memory that you place your attention.

Michelangelo is quoted as saying, "I saw an angel imprisoned within the marble so I carved until I set it free." In a very real sense you are that angel, imprisoned within the marble of your own self-limiting thoughts and feelings. This very simple process will allow you to chip away at those feelings, freeing you to be the person you've always wanted to be and to have the life that so far, you've only dreamed about.

Most people when told about the process don't believe that anything so simple, so uncomplicated, can work in the ways that I suggest. But I'm here to tell you that it does, and it will. You will become peaceful, centered and relaxed, and from that perspective you will find yourself enjoying life and happiness in ways that would have seemed impossible only a short time ago.

CHAPTER 1

What is Happiness?

"My life has no purpose, no direction, no aim, no meaning, and yet I'm happy. I can't figure it out. What am I doing right?"

—*CHARLES SCHULZ*

There are many books that have been published on ways to be more happy. There are tips, lists, philosophies and research on what makes people happy in cultures around the world. In fact, if you do an online search, you'll find different studies on which countries have the happiest people.

The challenge is that happiness is like the word *success* or *love*. There is no universal definition. Its meaning varies upon each of our interpretations. Yes, happiness may be attaining what each of us considers good, whether it's pleasure, contentment, peace or other feelings.

Perhaps one way to define happiness universally is that happiness is erasing or clearing away all of the things which cause us to feel unhappy. It's like clearing away the weeds to create a fertile area where flowers can easily blossom naturally.

The premise of this book is that happiness is your natural state of being. Happiness is already there underneath your *stuff*. By stuff, I mean all of the beliefs, feelings and other things that contribute to your unhappiness. Clear away the stuff and you'll allow your happiness to come forth. So the purpose of this book is to teach you an amazing, powerful yet simple way to clear away any blocks to happiness consciously, on cue. Welcome to the ZPoint Process.

CHAPTER 2

How the Process Was Created

"So I connected the dots."

—*ROBERT ALLEN*

It is my belief that everything in life is a process. For me, the process that culminated with the creation of The ZPoint Process began in the spring of 1999. At that time I was working in the computer department of Sir Sandford Fleming College in my home town of Peterborough, Ontario, Canada. I was a very unhappy person and was never satisfied by anything. I think I'd been that way all of my life.

I was filled with anger, resentment, a deep disappointment with my life and a bottomless longing for something more that I couldn't define. I can recall either being up or down or swinging somewhere between those two extremes. I can recall only a few times in my life to that point where I can honestly say that I was happy.

One day I came across a reference to a book about a fellow who claimed to have achieved enlightenment while serving a term in a Florida jail for selling drugs. The idea that this could happen under such conditions and circumstances intrigued me, so I immediately ordered the book. It was called *From Onions to Pearls*, by Satyam Nadeen.

There was something in that book that laid waste to every idea, belief and cherished notion that I had ever had. That book was a hand grenade thrown into a room filled with furniture, and the furniture was everything I believed and held to be true.

For some reason, the ideas in that book completely cleared away all of my old ways of being and left me bereft and adrift. I didn't know what to believe, what was right, what was wrong, what was up or what was down. I was a completely empty vessel.

For several months I wandered around completely oblivious to everything. I recall spending many hours sitting on my couch at home just staring off into space and just *being*. Gradually, I started rebuilding the furniture of my mind and my life began to make sense again. However, nothing was the same after that. I was different. I had changed.

Some months later, I *chanced* upon a website advertising an opportunity to become a Certified Hypnotherapist. I immediately remembered when I was a teenager, and the dreams I had for myself. There were three things I wanted more than anything: to write a book, to become "enlightened," and to learn hypnosis. I read everything I could about the latter two and trusted that one day I would write that book. This is the book.

I can recall buying a simple how-to book on hypnosis when I was fourteen and setting out to hypnotize my friends, sometimes with hilarious results. In late 1999, I fulfilled the dream of becoming a Hypnotherapist when I became certified by the National Guild of Hypnotists. My wife, the handy person in our family, converted our dining room into an office and I began seeing clients on a part-time basis.

My life continued to change, often in ways I could not have imagined. It became increasingly difficult for me to keep my mind focused on my job. It just didn't seem to fit me anymore. More and more, my thoughts became centered on becoming a full-time Hypnotherapist.

I started talking about leaving my job and devoting myself full time to my practice. Unfortunately, Peterborough is a relatively small place, and I wasn't earning enough to pay my way. My overwhelming desire for change led to a crisis within my marriage.

Quite often in our relationships we have unspoken contracts, shared goals, dreams and ways of being. When these ways of being change, as mine did so dramatically, seemingly stable relationships can reveal difficulties that lay buried beneath the surface.

One person wishes everything to remain the same while the other is moved inexorably along a different path in a different direction entirely. This is what happened to me. Sometimes love is not enough.

In the summer of 2003, I was sharing an apartment in a suburb of Toronto, earning a bare subsistence living as a full time Hypnotherapist, incorporating Emotional Freedom Techniques®(EFT®) and Tapas Acupressure Technique™ (TAT™) into my practice. Although financially things were difficult, emotionally and spiritually I was thriving.

The ups and downs were gone. Having said this, there were still deep issues I needed to resolve, and I was looking for a means to do this. I felt that I had gone as far as I could with EFT and TAT alone.

Around that time, I read *The Power of Now*, by Eckhart Tolle. That book had a huge impact on me. I practiced being in the *now* constantly and, after a while, could enter into the *now* state at will. I vividly recall how magical it was to simply walk down the street and watch the flowers and trees and suddenly my awareness would shift. Everything took on a life and a brilliance I'd never noticed before.

I'd walk to the Scarborough bluffs and spend hours sitting on a certain park bench overlooking Lake Ontario, just watching the clouds, the birds and the trees and drinking in the incredible beauty I saw spread before me. It was, as I've said, a magical time.

Right at this time, two things happened that changed my life. First, my flat-mate purchased the Larry Nims' *Be Set Free Fast* (BSFF) manual, and second, I read *Power vs.*

Force, by David R. Hawkins. I read Larry's manual and tried using BSFF, but somehow it didn't feel right to me. It is a brilliant piece of work, but it just didn't resonate with how I thought and especially how I felt. I'm very intuitive and approach everything from a feeling perspective. So I set it aside.

Then I read *Power vs. Force*. In it, Hawkins speaks about "Attractor Fields" or "M-fields." As I understood it, these are simply energetic patterns containing all of the possibilities inherent within an event, a circumstance or a condition. My life, for example, can be viewed in these terms. It is a large attractor field with my name on it.

Within that field are all of the smaller patterns that go to make up my thoughts, feelings and circumstances. Imagine an energetic bubble, within a bubble within a bubble. And, taken in ever broader terms, the world itself and the Universe and everything that exists, or has the potential of existing, does so within its own attractor field, one within the other. A wheel within a wheel within a wheel.

I was sitting in the washroom one night, where I often do my best thinking, and I suddenly put everything together. Attractor fields, how to adapt the cue word and *Cleaning Program* from BSFF and Eckhart Tolle's "pain-body." I saw how everything fit together so perfectly and so simply. Whole and complete. I saw it all in that one instant.

I was overwhelmed, and immediately set to work translating what I had seen into a usable process. I spent hours and hours trying this and trying that. I read a post on the BSFF e-mail list about the agreements we make with ourselves, and added this to the process. I read about the importance of forgiveness, and this too was added.

Friends would have an idea and we would try it out immediately. These were very exciting times. I spent many hours sitting on that park bench filled with the possibilities for the concept.

As I said when I began this story, everything is a process. Almost exactly a year later, after having used the original ZPoint Process on many people and having written the original manual, I had another idea. I was walking through High Park in Toronto, just enjoying my walk and decided to clear something that had been bothering me.

I started going through the process, which at this time was twelve or thirteen steps, when I found myself saying, "I clear all the ways I…" I paused and backtracked in my mind to what I had said to myself. I was astounded.

Again I saw the concept clearly—how to simplify the process and make it more effective at the same time. I didn't have paper and a pen with me, so I walked all the way home repeating, "I clear all the ways," over and over so I wouldn't forget it before I got home. And that is how the statement version was born.

I am very grateful to be the bearer of this process. I promise to always do my best to bring forth that which is given to me in trust for all of you.

CHAPTER 3

Book with Recordings

"A dimension of sound, a dimension of

sight, a dimension of mind."

—*ROD SERLING*

People learn best in multidimensional ways. That's why we've included some very special downloadable recordings with this book that will guide you through the ZPoint Process to release any difficult feelings that may plague you and instill a feeling of anticipation and excitement concerning whatever dreams you may have for yourself.

THE *GENERAL CLEARING* RECORDING

The *General Clearing* recording will guide you to let go of those feelings and beliefs that limit your health, your wealth and your personal happiness. Although it's only nine minutes long, the *General Clearing* recording will guide you through four separate ZPoint Processes to release whatever feeling you bring to it. You can download your personal copy of the *General Clearing* Recording and the *Creating New Possibilities* recording mentioned below by visiting the following link:

http://zpointforpeace.com/960906.shtml

Please note that I've also included a longer version of the *General Clearing* recording. If you find that you have extra time and wish to really relax, listening to the longer version will allow you to do so.

A little later in the book, I will show you how to evoke that "characteristic feeling" that represents all of the self-limiting beliefs connected to a particular issue, event or person. All you need do is feel that *characteristic feeling*, listen to the recording and repeat your cue word as you do so.

Because this recording is only nine minutes long, you can use it whenever you have a few minutes to spare, such as while commuting[1] or while relaxing after a difficult day. In fact, you can use it anywhere or anytime. You may want to load it onto your iPod or MP3 player and have it handy for such occasions.

---

1 For your safety, you are cautioned NOT to listen to the General Release recording while driving a vehicle or operating heavy machinery.

CREATING NEW POSSIBILITIES RECORDING

The *Creating New Possibilities* recording, only six minutes long, guides you through ZPoint "What if" statements to create a wonderful sense of expectancy and anticipation. This recording alone can very quickly shift you out of a bad mood to a place where you feel energized and hopeful.

It is well accepted that before we can change in a big way we must believe in that change and feel a sense of excitement and expectancy that it's on its way. Whenever you feel less than positive about where you are in your life, listening to this recording will fill you with a delicious sense of anticipation and excitement about your future.

It is also designed to let go of all the ways that you may block the realization of that future by releasing any inner resistance to having exactly what you want. There is an old saying that goes, "Where attention goes, energy flows."

When most or all of your attention is on what you don't want in life, energy flows to create more of that. What if by releasing the difficult feelings that currently hold your attention, you could allow yourself to feel good about your life and everything in it?

By using these recordings you will quickly shift your attention away from those things that make you feel bad, to things that make you feel good. And, following the rule that where attention goes, energy flows, you'll soon find those "good" feelings attracting even more good things into your life. Again, "It is never too late to be what you might have been." and you are about to discover the truth of that statement.

CHAPTER 4

How to Do the ZPoint Process

"Out of intense complexities

intense simplicities emerge."

—*WINSTON CHURCHILL*

The ZPoint Process itself is quite simple. In fact, you need concern yourself with only three things:

1. The *Cleaning Program.*
2. Choosing a special cue word to "activate" that program.
3. Placing your awareness on a what we call that *characteristic feeling* and releasing that feeling using the ZPoint Process.

THE *CLEANING PROGRAM*

The *Cleaning Program* is nothing more than a benign yet very powerful intention that you 'install' or set into your subconscious mind simply by reading a short paragraph of instructions. Once the program is installed you need never refer to it again and it will remain active for as long as you need it. Because the *Cleaning Program* is intended to allow us to realize our highest good, it always works in ways that bring us to a place of peace and emotional balance.

To activate the *Cleaning Program*, you repeat a special cue word. Cue words are like the on/off switch on a flashlight. When you notice an uncomfortable feeling connected to thoughts, memories or people in your experience, you point the beam of your awareness (your flashlight) in the direction you wish to shine the light of truth[2].

This act of pointing is the clearing statement. When you switch on your flashlight by repeating your cue word, the beam of your consciousness illuminates what needs to be released and the *Cleaning Program* does the rest. The cue word itself is simply a switch that activates the *Cleaning Program*. Although theoretically any word, phrase, sound or action will do, we prefer the word "yes." *Yes* always feels good when you say it.

---

2 There are truths and there are beliefs. Truths we share with the whole of humanity. Beliefs, although they may be shared, are peculiar to each individual.

REPEATING YOUR CUE WORD

Recently, I had a call from someone who was using the ZPoint Process instructions with a friend over the phone. They would meet once a week and share the clearing statements. After two months they weren't having much success. One of the women actually gave up and slipped into depression. After speaking with the first woman for a few minutes, I found out she was only saying her cue word once after each statement. As the saying goes, "once is not enough."

This is especially true with ZPoint. Repeating your cue with intention in conjunction with the *Cleaning Program* sets up a specific resonance within your subconscious mind. The more focused you are on simply repeating your cue word and being very present as you do so, the more effective that resonance and ZPoint will be.

One of the reasons I created *Allowing Happiness on Cue* was because the process is simply more effective when someone guides you through the statements. This leaves you free to place your awareness squarely on the simple repetition of your cue word thereby creating that resonance that I spoke of earlier.

JUST LIKE A COMPUTER

For those of you who are computer literate, you may find it helpful to think of the ZPoint Process in computer terms. In a very real sense, the *Cleaning Program* acts just like a master computer program that "cleans" the hard drive of damaged or malicious programming.

To delete such programming, you would merely focus the light of your awareness on that feeling that you wish to release, listen to the *General Clearing* recording, and repeat your cue word until the feeling no longer troubles you. As you do this, you will find yourself slipping into a wonderfully relaxed state as the conflicted programming is cleaned or released entirely.

If you are unsure of which cue word to use, again I suggest using the word *yes*. In effect you are saying *yes* to life every time you repeat that word to yourself. Remember, you can always change it later simply by saying, "I change my cue word to _____." Because your subconscious mind remembers and responds to everything you do, say, think or feel, it will immediately take effect.

THE ZPOINT SUBCONSCIOUS CLEANING PROGRAM

Now, to begin, please read the instructions in italics below aloud to yourself:

I hereby set a powerful intention within you, my subconscious mind, to affect the best of all possible outcomes by this clearing, and each time I notice a feeling that does not feel good as I think certain thoughts or remember certain people, situations or events, you will gently and easily eliminate that feeling completely as I repeat my cue word over and over, and you will eliminate every-thing I feel because of it, everything I feel that connects to it and everything I feel that has resulted from it, to whatever extent it exists within me.

ZPOINT STATEMENTS

Now, having installed the *Cleaning Program* and cho-sen a cue word, you are ready to begin freeing yourself from the feelings and patterns of behavior that are not in alignment with living a more abundant and fulfilled life. To do this, you need only focus your attention on that uncomfortable feeling that arises as you think about an issue, concern or memory that troubles you and listen to the *General Clearing* recording while repeating your cue word like a mantra until the discomfort is gone. It's really quite simple.

To facilitate our focusing on these uncomfortable feelings, we use specially designed "clearing" statements. I think of the ZPoint Process as an Intention Multiplier, where each aspect of the ZPoint Process works together to release difficult feelings in much the same way a mag-nifying glass and the sun will produce fire on a sunny day.

ZPoint works in exactly the same way as it signifi-cantly enhances and magnifies your Intention to perma-nently release whatever it is that troubles you. In a very real sense ZPoint is a spiritual technology, and all that it requires of you is your willingness to apply it.

CLEARING THE WAYS

When you say the words, "I clear[3] all the ways I feel this feeling," you are instructing your subconscious mind and the *Cleaning Program* to release all of the possible ways that you feel or experience a particular feeling and the unconscious beliefs connected to it. Our experiences and the beliefs they engender, are always connected or associated with other memories or feelings within the database of our unconscious self.

The common factor here is the feeling we experience as we think certain thoughts or remember certain events. That feeling, whether good or bad, is an emotional or energetic representation of the beliefs that give it life. It's like a red flare shot into the air every time we think that thought or remember that person, event or situation.

---

3 To *Clear* as used with the ZPoint Process is to make transparent, to clean, to reveal the truth whatever that may be.

CHAPTER 5

Clearing Limiting Thoughts, Beliefs

"Human beings have used their incredible abilities to develop a staggering array of limiting beliefs, justifications and excuses for every occasion. What a waste!"

—ROBERT WHITE

Thinking thoughts that limit you in some way will always produce feelings that don't feel good as you think them. On the other hand, remembering pleasant events or thinking life-affirming thoughts will produce feelings that always feel good as you think them.

BELIEFS ARE ENERGETIC PATTERNS

Beliefs like all thoughts are nothing more than energetic patterns and each has a specific energy signature. Similar beliefs have similar signatures and these appear to cluster together forming larger and larger energetic patterns. Like attracts like.

I'm sure you've noticed that when you think a thought or remember an event, that memory will often trigger other memories, which in turn trigger more thoughts and then even more thoughts. It's like pulling a loose thread from a sweater. That thread is connected to other threads, which are connected to other threads, and those threads are connected to even more threads. And the common factor is always that *characteristic feeling* that arises as we think certain thoughts.

With ZPoint, we always work from the most general aspects of a situation to the specific. In releasing that *characteristic feeling* using the ZPoint Process we affect not only the obvious issue at hand, we also affect any other issues that may be connected to it just like the loose threads in the sweater mentioned above. In this way, if you release a feeling on a very general level as suggested, you will often find that the results appear in unexpected and always pleasing ways.

For example, if you are working on your anger at a relative, you may find not only has your anger toward that relative disappeared, you also find yourself no longer responding with anger in other seemingly unrelated situations. That anger toward your relative was related to other ways that you became angry and when you cleared *all the ways* you grow angry, you unknowingly released those others as well.

CLEARING PATTERNS

Patterns, are prerecorded, choreographed responses we have to certain situations or triggers. Life is a complex affair, and to survive we often find ourselves responding to certain situations with automatic learned behavior. If someone says hello to us, we normally respond by saying hello back to them. We don't think about this, we respond quite automatically.

This unthinking, unconscious pre-recorded response to certain situations can cause us to take actions that we may regret later. For example, in the 1970s, a religious sect, the Hare Krishnas stumbled upon an ingenious means of soliciting money at airports and public places that proved to be wildly successful. One of their members would walk up to you and pin a small flower to your lapel and then ask for a donation.

Their method takes advantage of the fact that we will respond unthinkingly in certain specific circumstances, in this case, people giving us a gift. Most people responded to the Hare Krishnas by giving money, even when they really didn't want to. Many did so without questioning what they were doing because we are taught from an early age to respond in this way.

While not everyone responds by returning the gift, enough did to make the Hare Krishnas very wealthy indeed. You will see the same mechanism in place when a company hands out free samples in your local grocery store. Again, not everyone returns the favor, but enough will to make the effort worthwhile.

We are programmed by our society to return a gift with a gift or a favor for a favor. In fact, our society would literally cease to function if this social programming wasn't in place.

Some people no doubt felt good when they returned the Hare Krishna's gift with a donation while an increasing number of others did not. How often do you find yourself responding to a request and don't feel good as you are doing so, but say yes anyway? Does it feel good to say yes on those occasions? No, I didn't think so.

RELEASE THAT PATTERN

What if you could release that pattern of automatically responding to the demands of others in ways that don't serve you or make you feel guilty? In effect, that learned behavior is making your decisions for you. When we give, it feels far better to give with an open heart than from a guilty one.

Spending a few minutes using the ZPoint Process and focusing on that *characteristic feeling* that comes up as you recall those situations will release your need to respond automatically. You can then choose, with conscious awareness, whether to say yes or no to the request depending on how you feel at that moment. You will have taken back conscious control from the pattern. You will begin making better choices that serve not only your higher interest, but the higher interest of everyone involved.

RELEASING DISEMPOWERING BELIEFS

Each day we have thousands of thoughts, and each one of these thoughts is based on what we believe to be true about a situation, circumstance or relationship. So, when we have a thought, that thought, with its underlying set of beliefs or assumptions, is connected to a corresponding emotion that represents *all* of the beliefs that underlie it.

If that thought is one of personal empowerment, the emotion associated with it always feels good as we think it. If that thought is disempowering in some way, the associated emotion will always make us feel bad in that moment. Try this out for yourself and see.

Below are a list of common words. Allow yourself to be aware of the feeling that each word evokes within you:

- Home
- Father
- Sunshine
- Sex
- Marriage

Each word represents a thought or concept and that concept will evoke a feeling. That feeling depends on the belief or feeling associations that you have with that word. If the word doesn't feel good to you, you are holding the energy of untruth behind the thought, and this can be released with the ZPoint Process. When you do this, you release any limiting beliefs connected to that feeling.

Because of this energetic connection between emotions and beliefs, our emotions become an easily identified representation of the beliefs we hold. Remembering that many of these beliefs are largely unexamined or unconscious, uncomfortable feelings can guide us to areas where we may hold beliefs that prevent us from finding personal happiness and fulfillment.

And because we focus on the feeling rather than the belief itself, we don't need to know specifically what those disempowering beliefs are in order to transform them. We need only feel that feeling and release it using the ZPoint Process thereby causing the attached beliefs to transform themselves.

If a thought feels good, you can be assured that the beliefs you hold in this area are life-affirming ones. If a thought feels bad, you can also be assured that your beliefs in this area are self-limiting in some way. They actually prevent you from living a happier, healthier, more abundant and more fulfilling life.

The emotions we feel are like little batteries that hold particular thoughts or belief structures in place. So, when we release the uncomfortable feelings connected to these thoughts, it not only releases that uncomfortable feeling, it also causes any beliefs associated to them to be transformed as well. Thoughts of *I can't* are transformed into thoughts of *I can.*

FILL IN THE BLANKS STATEMENTS

One very interesting characteristic of the subconscious mind is that it works by association. In other words, it associates each memory stored within it with other memories that are similar in some way. You may have noticed this yourself when you remember an event, thought or feeling and that act of remembering leads you to other memories, thoughts or feelings, one after the other. Some of these associations may seem obvious, while others appear to be quite unrelated to the original thought.

For example, if you to think of a pink elephant, the very act of thinking that thought will lead you to other thoughts and to still more thoughts. Following the chain of those thoughts can lead to some very interesting places, many of which can seem totally unrelated to the original thought of a pink elephant. Nonetheless, your subconscious has linked or associated these thoughts in ways that it understands and can easily and instantly access.

A LARGE DATABASE

In all the ways that matter, our subconscious mind is very similar to a very large database where every experience, thought or feeling you've ever had is stored. And, it appears that the common factor or key to this database is in the feeling we feel as we think certain thoughts.

Fill in the blank statements make use of this characteristic and freely associate words, concepts and feelings with other words, concepts and feelings already stored within that database. One way of saying statements would be:

> ➤ *I clear all the ways I become upset whenever my boss yells at me. <yes>*

The *Cleaning Program*, when activated by the cue word, would instantly associate subconscious patterns where you become upset when your boss yells at you. However, a much more profound way would be to clear every pattern where you become upset no matter what the cause. You could do this with the following fill in the blanks statements:

> ➤ *I clear all the ways I grow upset because... <yes>*
> ➤ *I clear all the ways I grow upset whenever... <yes>*
> ➤ *I clear all the ways I may grow upset if... <yes>*

Notice how we leave the ending blank. In doing so, you allow your subconscious mind to search through all the ways you become upset and release it. I think you'll find that the results you achieve will generalize into many different areas of your life.

In using the *because* variable, your subconscious will find and delete the many possible reasons you become upset, and it does so beneath your normal conscious awareness. In effect, it releases all of the possible ways you've been programmed to respond to specific situations by unconsciously acting out certain self limiting or self sabotaging behaviors.

It is important to understand that it does so without any conscious effort or direction on your part. It's a process, and you set it in motion the moment you decide to release whatever feeling you put your attention on and begin repeating your cue word.

A LOST BICYCLE RACE

Many years ago, when I was about eleven, I entered my hometown's Labor Day bicycle race. I had a brand new ten-speed bicycle and I could ride like the wind. I started off very quickly and soon was leading the half mile race.

For some unknown reason as I neared the finish line I slowed down and stopped pedaling. I wanted to win and yet some interior thought told me that I'd already crossed the finish line, when actually I hadn't. In the next instant a dozen riders flashed passed me and I finished dead last.

What was it that told me to stop pedaling? What was it that led me to believe that I had already crossed the finish line when clearly I hadn't? When I look back, I believe it was my internal programming that *couldn't see me as a winner* and so distracted me into losing the race. How many times have you done something similar in your own life?

What we believe to be true about ourselves will be played out in our life experience. If deep down you believe yourself to be a loser as I did, you will sabotage yourself whenever you have the opportunity to stand out and shine. The heartbreaking part is that no one does this to us. We do it to ourselves!

CHAPTER 6

Clearing Limiting Memories, Feelings

"At first it was hard to let go, but now I

expect change. It's part of life."

—*AJ ANAGNOS*

The ZPoint *Erase the Tape* method grew out of my desire to completely release the effect of painful memories in my life. Like all things ZPoint, it's very simple to use and to get wonderful results every time.

ETT STEPS

Imagine a light filled circle in front of you. Now imagine taking all of the difficult feelings you have toward yourself and others, along with any feelings connected or associated with any memories associated with those feelings, and imagine placing them in the circle to be returned to the pure undifferentiated energy they were created from.

To accomplish this you need only count down from 10 to zero while repeating your cue over and over like a mantra. If you find it helpful, you can think of ETT (Erase the Tape) as a spiritual cleansing and recycling program that takes any thought, feeling or belief not based in truth and returns it to its original source.

As you count down slowly from 10 to zero while repeating your cue between each count, you may become aware of the uncomfortable thoughts and feelings your subconscious associates back to the original *characteristic feeling* you brought to the circle. Many people report remembering long forgotten situations or circumstances from early childhood that caused those difficult feelings in the first place. Others report feeling body aches or pains that are brought up to be released in the circle. Whatever your experience, you will notice a distinct feeling of release and peace when you complete your countdown.

Another aspect of ETT is the empty circle. It is said that the whole of creation is separated into the seen and the unseen, the known and the unknown. Imagining an empty circle can be looked upon as a window into the unseen world where any unseen elements that may have the effect of your keeping that *characteristic feeling* in place may be found. Again, you don't need to know what those elements are, you need only intend that those unseen or unknown things be released as you count down slowly from 10 to zero while repeating your cue between counts.

WHAT IF STATEMENTS

Another powerful aspect of ZPoint are what I call *What if?* statements. A few years ago as I was in the process of developing ZPoint to what it is now, my financial situation was precarious to say the least. Because of this, I was forced to take temporary jobs to pay the bills. One of those temporary jobs was working for a top real estate agent here in Toronto. His name was Richard Dougal and he was simply an amazing salesperson.

Richard taught me the value of asking simple questions rather than making declarative statements. Questions seldom generate resistance to the message they carry and so are more readily and easily accepted by inner portions of our self.

For example, a simple affirmation would be, "Every day in every way I get better and better." This affirmation if repeated often enough will shift your perception of yourself and allow positive change.

The only problem with this approach is that it can take a very long time before your subconscious mind accepts this affirmation as a statement of truth. You may need to repeat it hundreds and hundreds of times before you get past your mind's resistance to accepting it as fact.

IT'S ALL ABOUT RESISTANCE

Questions on the other hand do not generate this resistance. Try this for yourself right now. Repeat the following two statements and allow yourself to become aware of the feeling that arises as you do so.

- *Every day, in every way I get better and better.*

  Or,

- *What if every day, in every way, I do get better and better?*

Which one feels better to you? My guess is that it will be the second one. There is little or no resistance to this affirmation when offered in the form of a question. This means that your subconscious will accept it as truth much faster.

Now, say the *what if* again, this time repeating your cue for 10 seconds afterward.

➤ *What if every day, in every way, I do get better and better. <yes>*

Do you feel the difference? Does this feel even better?

According to all the best spiritual teachers, when we release our resistance to having a thing, and feel a sense of anticipation believing that we will get it, that thing will flow to us. "What if every day, in every way, I do get better and better?"

You can measure your resistance to allowing anything simply by being aware of how you feel as you think of it. Feeling good as you think about it means there no resistance to your realizing your desire and you can now rest easy and stop struggling. It's on its way!

LISTENING TO *CREATING NEW POSSIBILITIES*

The second recording included with this book is titled *Creating New Possibilities*. The affirmations you will hear are all stated in the form of a question. They are very general in nature and will affect broad issues that may concern everyone.

I think you'll find that listening to this recording will not only make you feel great in the moment, the *what ifs* I speak on your behalf are designed to create that sense of anticipation and excitement I spoke about earlier. You may listen to the recording over and over until that feeling extends into all parts of your life. These are precisely the feelings required to allow whatever it is that you really want into your everyday experience.

Whenever you need a quick dose of positive feeling just listen to this recording, repeating your cue after each statement. The recording is only six minutes long and can be listened to anywhere. No matter how busy your life, most people can find six minutes to shift to a much more positive mood. You'll be glad you did, and so will everyone around you.

What if every time you do this, you create new possibilities for health, wealth and happiness where none existed before?

CLEARING THE WAYS TO FEELING GOOD

And now we get to the core of the issue. In this section you will be guided to release that *characteristic feeling* that arises as you think of or remember those parts of your life that trouble you in some way.

Remember, it's not necessary to know why these things happened or why you carry these difficult feelings, it's only necessary to feel them and know that they are there. It's about releasing negative feelings and allowing your happiness to shine through. An understanding of the whys will usually come later, after you've released that *characteristic feeling*.

For example, when you think about your childhood, is there a feeling that comes up as soon as you think of it? Most people do and if it's not a good feeling, that feeling will seem quite old. After all, you've been carrying it around for a long time.

Just allow yourself to feel that feeling and mark it with your awareness. You needn't try to put a name to it, as this tends to limit the results of your clearing. Although you may say to yourself that you feel sad or angry when you remember your childhood, allow yourself to just feel that feeling and let it be whatever it is without putting a name to it.

A handy statement to use to evoke that *characteristic feeling* would be, "Whenever I think about _____, I feel..." leaving the ending blank to allow the subconscious to target all of the feelings involved.

In our example, we are intending to release that *characteristic feeling* that comes up as you think of your childhood as a whole. Therefore, the statement we would use would be:

> ➤ *Whenever I think about my childhood, I feel... <yes>*

You would then repeat your cue word, which in this case would be *yes* like a mantra for about 10 seconds. During this time you would begin to play the *General Release* recording to release that *characteristic feeling* completely. As you are doing this, many of the self-limiting beliefs you acquired during this period of your life are released or transformed, leaving you feeling peaceful and relaxed.

GENERAL CLEARING

As in the above example, think about your life to this point and read the following statement to yourself remembering to repeat your cue as you do so.

> ➤ *Whenever I think about my life, I feel... <yes>*

MARK THAT FEELING AND RELEASE IT

Mark that feeling as it arises and listen to the *General Release* recording remembering to repeat your cue as you do so. Thoughts, images, memories or the awareness of body sensations may come into your mind as you listen and that's okay. It is just your subconscious bringing these things up where they can be released. Just be the observer and continue repeating your cue after each statement.

As you listen to the recording you may find yourself yawning deeply. This is typically an indication that the ZPoint Process is working. Some people, myself included, find their eyes tearing, or experience sensations in their body. This too indicates that the ZPoint Process is doing what it was intended to do. Just allow this and continue repeating your cue word.

IT'S ALL ABOUT THE FEELING

Once you've played the recording to the end, pay attention to how you feel. You'll quickly learn how to judge whether you can move on the next *characteristic feeling* by how relaxed you are inside. There is a particular feeling that comes when you have completely released everything connected to what you were working on. Your mind will be clear but very quiet and you will feel very peaceful inside.

I've noticed this effect in everyone I've worked with as well as with myself. Long time meditators who use the ZPoint Process believe that state to be one of deep meditation where all is quiet and incessant thoughts are stilled.

Most people report feeling lighter and sometimes even taller. Many feel energy moving throughout their body. Some have true spiritual experiences. Whatever happens always feels good. There is no mistaking this when it happens to you.

If you don't feel that feeling as I describe, simply listen to the recording one more time. There will be a new *characteristic feeling* that represents the remainder of the first *characteristic feeling* and your resistance to letting it go. Take that feeling with you as you listen to the recording again.

Some people report feeling fatigued after listening to the recording. This too is an indication that you are releasing at a very deep level. The fatigue will generally pass within a few minutes leaving you energized and alert. If you wish, and if circumstances permit, take a short nap. I think you'll find it will work wonders.

If it persists, feel that *characteristic feeling* associated with that tiredness and use the recording to release it. Just feel that tired feeling and play your recording.

EVOKING THAT *CHARACTERISTIC FEELING*

Whenever we evoke that *characteristic feeling* and release it, we also release any self limiting beliefs that may be connected to it. When this happens we are suddenly able to see that particular issue or relationship from a different perspective. It's like we can't see the forest for the trees, and in releasing those former limiting beliefs and attitudes we rise above the issue and perceive it differently.

Where before we may have perceived only the problems connected to that issue, now we are able to shift our focus to aspects of the situation where we can make a fresh choice. Often that choice is simply to let it go and no longer worry about it. Or, we can suddenly see ways to resolve the situation in ways that empower everyone involved, including ourselves.

GENERAL LIFE CLEARINGS

You'll notice that the first set of clearings deal with releasing unconscious attitudes and beliefs from certain specific periods of our lives. You may find it helpful to think of this as a general house cleaning where your intention is to simply sweep the floor, dust and throw out items that shouldn't be there. Although we will focus on specific issues later in the book, at this point we simply want to get rid of the background clutter at a very general level.

It's very important to remember that you really can't get this wrong. It's all about your intention to do something positive about your life right now. That overall intention will allow the ZPoint Process to do its job no matter how perfectly or poorly you think you are doing this.

Many people are used to things being complicated and difficult. Bear this in mind as you work through the following clearings. If you think you may be doing something wrong, just stop for a moment and remind yourself how easy this whole thing really is. Just feel the feeling and listen to the recording. Trust that the process will work as intended, and it will.

RELEASING CLUTTER FROM THE PAST

What follows are opening statements intended to bring up that *characteristic feeling* that energetically represents certain periods of your life. Remember, that feeling is connected to much of the conflicted programming that may be causing you to live anything less than a wonderful life right now.

My suggestion would be to start with the first statement, be aware that just reading the statement will bring up the *characteristic feeling* that energetically represents that period of time. At this point you would play the *General Clearing* recording and release it and everything that is not the truth connected to it.

While some people may wish to dive in and do all of the clearings at one shot, I would recommend that you take a more leisurely approach. Do the first clearing and allow yourself to sit with it for a while.

Allow yourself to enjoy the peace of mind and happiness that comes from using ZPoint in this way. Think back to that time again and allow yourself to remember the good things that happened, even the smallest of good things. Make peace with this time in your life. Then move on to the next statement.

➤ *When I remember my life to age five, I feel... <yes>*
➤ *When I remember my life from age six to 12, I feel... <yes>*
➤ *When I remember my teenage years, I feel... <yes>*

- ➤ *When I remember my twenties (thirties, forties, etc.) I feel... <yes>*
- ➤ *When I think about this time in my life, I feel... <yes>*
- ➤ *When I think about my future, I feel... <yes>*
- ➤ *When I think about my past, I feel... <yes>*

Remember, if you don't feel completely peaceful after completing each statement, think of that time again and listen to the recording one more time.

BEING MORE SPECIFIC

The purpose of the foregoing exercise was to clear away the clutter in much the same way that you would clear away the trash from an open lot you intend to build on. Then you know what you're dealing with. The following clearings are intended to release the pain and accumulated upset around specific circumstances and situations in your current life today. You may find it helpful to tell yourself a story about these specific situations.

For example, what is the story you tell yourself about your current money situation? Just say to yourself, "I don't have money because..." and list all the becauses. Because I'm not smart enough, or because I need more education, or because they won't let me or because he won't listen to me. The list can go on and on. These are your reasons why you don't have enough money and all will evoke that *characteristic feeling* that we're looking for.

Make up a story for each of these statements and check each one after listening to your recording. If the reasons you wrote don't now seem untrue, listen to the recording again.

Let's start with the first statement.

➤ *When I think about my money situation, I feel... <yes>*

➤ *When I think about how hard I work (or can't work), I feel... <yes>*

➤ *When I think about my job (or lack thereof) I feel... <yes>*

➤ *When I think about doing work I love, I feel... <yes>*

➤ *When I think about the world (or national) situation, I feel... <yes>*

➤ *When I think about my boss, I feel... <yes>*

➤ *When I think about my in-laws, I feel... <yes>*

➤ *When I think about my children, I feel... <yes>*

➤ *When I think about my parents, I feel... <yes>*

➤ *When I think about embarrassing myself in public, I feel... <yes>*

➤ *When I think about my (failed) marriage(s), I feel... <yes>*

➤ *When I think about my failures, I feel... <yes>*

➤ *When I think about my mistakes, I feel... <yes>*

➤ *When I think about (a specific circumstance), I feel... <yes>*

- ➤ *When I think about my burdens, I feel... <yes>*
- ➤ *Whenever I think about my health, I feel... <yes>*
- ➤ *Whenever I remember that time I _____, I feel... <yes>*
- ➤ *When I think of being irritated, I feel... <yes>*
- ➤ *When I think about being stressed, I feel... <yes>*
- ➤ *When I think about what stresses me, I feel... <yes>*
- ➤ *When I think about being overwhelmed, I feel... <yes>*
- ➤ *When I think about what I have bottled up inside, I feel... <yes>*
- ➤ *When I think about losing _____, I feel... <yes>*
- ➤ *When I think about failing, I feel... <yes>*
- ➤ *When I think about being wildly successful, I feel... <yes>*
- ➤ *When I think about being humiliated, I feel... <yes>*
- ➤ *When I remember lost opportunities, I feel... <yes*
- ➤ *When I think about all the times I wanted to say something, but didn't, I feel... <yes>*
- ➤ *When I think about all the times I judged myself or others too harshly, I feel... <yes>*
- ➤ *When I remember being unsafe, I feel... <yes>*

If you haven't already done so, try some of the statements above and listen to the recording after doing so. I would suggest you read through the statements and run the ZPoint Process on those that you feel drawn to or repelled by.

Allow this to be easy and effortless and it will be. Release everything and anything from your experience that doesn't feel good as you think of it. The more you do this, the lighter and happier you will become.

There may be times when you feel little or nothing when you use the above statements. None of us like to feel bad and we can sometimes distance ourselves from our true feelings and suppress them. The process will work anyway. It will release that *characteristic feeling* whether or not you can actually feel it. You've set the intention to do so and the ZPoint Process takes care of the rest.

CHAPTER 7

Healing Relationships

"It is amazing to see how much we act like mirrors to each other in our relationships."

—*MADAN KATARIA*

We can the heal the present by marking "paid" to the past. We all have relationships with difficult people. Whenever we think about these people we become angry or sad or very upset. I'd like to tell you the story of my relationship with my twin sister. It illustrates beautifully how using this process can alter those relationships in ways that affect not only you, but the person you are in conflict with.

MY SISTER AND I

I love my sister, but from a very early age we would fight like cats and dogs at the drop of a hat. If we found ourselves in the same room it would only take a few minutes before we were at each other's throats. We'd both try to be pleasant, but we couldn't seem to find a way to move past these difficult feelings to allow true communication.

After creating the original *Relationships Protocol*, I decided to use it on myself after one particularly difficult conversation that I had with her. At the time the protocol[4] required me to individually clear all the anger, judgment, criticism, blame, shame and unforgivingness that I carried in my heart toward her. I just let it all go and afterward I felt good when I thought of her.

The very next day she called and not once during our conversation was I triggered in the slightest way. I remained calm and centered throughout and responded with warmth and love. It was amazing. And, what was most surprising to me, she wasn't triggered by me either. I realized later that it takes two to tango and when one of you stops the music, the dance stops for both of you.

Since then, we've spoken many times and I feel I have my sister back. Although I loved her before just because she was my sister, I took pains to avoid her. Now I find myself actually enjoying our time together.

WHEN WE HEAL A RELATIONSHIP

We are all connected. When we change ourselves, our world changes with us and that includes the people in

---

4 ZPoint remains a work in progress. The characteristic feeling method applied to relationships as used in this book and recording is a development of the original *Relationships Protocol* that I used with my sister.

our experience. They respond to us differently because using the ZPoint Process removes the trigger in us that corresponds to a similar trigger in them. This allows the truth to be known about that relationship and that truth is always one of love or compassion and sometimes both.

Shortly after experiencing the power of the ZPoint Process to transform my relationship with my sister, I decided to run the ZPoint Process on all of my relationships, even the ones from my past. I started out with a long list of names with the name of my father at the top. When I finished, I realized just how much those past hurts and humiliations defined who I thought I was.

I defined myself by how those others viewed me and I realized that their view was skewed by the former negative emotional patterns we shared. Once those feelings were gone, I was free to see myself in a much more accepting, compassionate and loving way. And so will you.

Another strange thing happened. The past became totally irrelevant to me. It's not that I don't remember everything that's happened to me, it's just that I'm no longer even remotely interested in remembering much of that past. The difficult feelings are gone leaving only a sense of peace and completion. In other words, all debts are paid. This leaves me free to put all my attention on what's happening now, and now is where our true power to create a wonderful life lies.

So, if you wish to do the same, if you wish to make peace with your past, you can start by making a top 10 list of those people in your life, both past and present, who when you think of them, evoke a feeling that is uncomfortable in some way.

You may find it very helpful to estimate your level of distress when you think about each person. On a scale of zero to 10, with 10 being the most intense, what level of distress does each person evoke within you? Just mark it down beside each name. You'll be able to use those numbers later to tell you how you're doing with your list.

Don't worry that in clearing these feelings, you may somehow erase what is good about those relationships. When we 'clear' a relationship we release everything that is not the truth. Love is always the highest truth and cannot be erased or released. In surrendering those relationships to the ZPoint Process, you are actually clearing all the ways you resist that truth in some way. The end result is that you find yourself loving and understanding them even more.

Now, take the first person on your list and begin:

➤ *Whenever I think about _____, I feel... <yes>*

As you repeat your cue, switch on your *General Release* recording and release the *characteristic feeling* that energetically represents your relationship with that person. And when you're done, just bring that person to mind again and see if those difficult feelings are gone. Remember what I said about recognizing when it's completely gone.

As you proceed through your list using exactly the same steps as above, go back each time and re-estimate your level of distress with each remaining person. You may find it interesting to watch those numbers change, even before you process them.

Finally, put your own name down on your list. Estimate your level of distress as you think about yourself.

And then:

➤ *Whenever I think about myself, I feel... <yes>*

Then listen to the recording.

CHAPTER 8

Let's Get Physical

"Our own physical body possesses a wisdom which we who inhabit the body lack. We give it orders which make no sense."

—HENRY MILLER

If you were to look in a mirror right now, how do you think you'd feel? Would you feel good about how you look? Would you feel good about yourself?

RELEASING BODY AND OTHER ISSUES

This is perhaps the easiest and yet most profound exercise in this book. It involves you simply standing in front of a mirror and looking at your reflection as you play the *General Clearing* recording. A hand mirror will do, but a full length mirror would be best.

As you look at your reflection in the mirror, what is the first feeling that comes up to your awareness? That is the *characteristic feeling*. Mark it with your awareness and switch on the recording. You can then sit down and listen as the recording guides you to release that feeling.

Each time you look into the mirror you will see a different aspect of yourself. Our intention is to release those aspects that don't please you until like Michelangelo's Angel, you see yourself as whole, complete and beautiful!

Initially, you may find this difficult to do, however that resistance will soon pass and as you use this technique more often you will very quickly find yourself actually liking who you see reflected in the mirror. The key is to come to that place where you like what you see and according to the Law of Attraction, when you feel good about yourself you will attract the circumstances that will begin to change your body in ways that will align with that new image of yourself.

When you look into the mirror, how does your image make you feel? Those feelings are your guide. If you don't like those feelings, if they don't feel good as you look at yourself, please know that you now have a powerful tool to help you change them. Just feel that feeling and play the *General Release* recording as you do so.

Our bodies are a perfect reflection of the deep inner beliefs we unconsciously hold about ourselves. When we see ourselves as dumpy or frumpy or fat, it is because this is the reflection of who we believe ourselves to be. But what if you change those deep inner beliefs and begin to view yourself differently?

WHAT WEIGHS ON YOU?

If you are overweight, look into the mirror and feel for any anger at your current situation. Many people report that once they released the anger, their weight just started to fall away. They found themselves eating better and felt the need to snack on unhealthy or starchy foods less often. They didn't think about this. It just happened.

When my wife and I split in 2001, I weighed just over 270 pounds. I needed a belt and a pair of suspenders to keep my pants up. At this moment, I weight a comfortable 210 pounds. I didn't set out to lose the weight. It just happened.

In fact, the first week after leaving I noticed that I had lost almost 10 pounds. Only later did I come to realize that in removing myself from that situation, I no longer felt compelled to overeat as a means of comforting myself from the feelings of anger and deep frustration that the marriage brought up in me.

It is important to note that I am not suggesting you should leave your spouse. I am suggesting however that you leave your anger and other difficult feelings behind using the recordings that come with this book. And when you do this, it is almost certain that you will begin to see yourself and your life differently and that difference will sooner or later be reflected in your mirror for all to see.

Many people overeat not from hunger, but from a need to fill an emptiness or void within. What do you think would happen if the next time you felt that particular feeling, you marked it in your awareness and listened to your recording?

What if you can let that feeling go and eat only when you're really hungry? Below you'll find some additional *What if* statements that should help you with this process of inner and outer change.

- ➤ *What if I can come to love and accept myself, just the way I am? <yes>*
- ➤ *What if in accepting myself and how I look right now, I set in motion the circumstances that will lead me to be more fully the person I've always wanted to be? <yes>*
- ➤ *What if I can let go of the extra weight? <yes>*
- ➤ *What if I can become beautiful in my own eyes and in the eyes of all who meet me? <yes>*
- ➤ *What if every day, in every way, I do get better and better? <yes>*
- ➤ *What if every day, in every way, I come to love myself and my life more and more? <yes>*
- ➤ *What if...? <yes>*

EXERCISING WITH ZPOINT

I enjoy walking. Not only is it good exercise, it gets you out of your head and into the *now* as you pay attention to what's going on around you.

One way to combine your ZPoint with exercise is to carry the clearing recording with you in an MP3 player or iPod. As you walk or exercise, play the recording and repeat your cue with each step. If you have a particular issue that concerns you, set the intention that it be released as you exercise. If you have no particular issue in mind, just allow those thoughts and feelings that naturally arise to guide your clearing and enjoy the wonderful feeling of relaxation that naturally occurs.

This can be done for any type of exercise. All you need is your iPod and a desire to become more peaceful, centered and relaxed.

Another very effective way of doing this is to simply repeat your cue word as you exercise. Just repeating your cue word alone will often shift negative ways of thinking in difficult or awkward situations. Many people who use the ZPoint Process often find themselves automatically repeating their cue in these moments and quickly return to a state of balance. Really, it's easy to do this and the results can often be astonishing.

CHAPTER 9

More Happiness Tools

"Let your hopes, not your hurts,

shape your future."

—*ROBERT H. SCHULLER*

In an ideal world we would only need to ask for whatever we want and the Universe would respond by giving it to us, immediately. However, have you noticed that most often we get what we don't seem to want? We don't want to be financially challenged, and yet most of us are. We don't want to be sick and yet it seems that many have sickness in abundance. We don't want to work at jobs we hate, and yet many of us do exactly that.

CLEANING UP THE BUTS

We say to ourselves, "I want to have the money to buy the things that will make my life easier." We hear ourselves ask for this and then when it doesn't promptly show up we say that God has forsaken us or that He doesn't exist or that the Law of Attraction doesn't work.

However, when we ask for something, we're not listening to what we're really asking for, and it goes something like this. "I want to have the money to buy the things to make my life easier", and if you listen closely you'll hear a big *BUT* tacked onto the end of our request.

"I want the money, *BUT* I'd need to work a few extra hours to get it, or, the government would only take most of it in tax anyway, or, I just never seem to get what I want." It always feels good to think about having extra money, *but* there always seems to be an under-thought that finishes our sentences with a big *but*, and those thoughts never feel good when we think them.

When we ask for anything we're sending a signal to the Universe that says, "Give me this!" Our desire for anything is a call to the Universe that says, "Hey Universe, this is what I want" and the Universe says, "Where shall I put it?"

Blocked desire on the other hand says "I really want this, *but.*" The Universe, always our faithful provider says, "Your wish is my command," and gives you the *but* of your desire. The *but* is whatever it is that follows the original request. You literally get that. *Buts* negate that part of the request that you really want.

Take a moment and think of something you want, but has eluded you. That's right, there's always a big *but* in there somewhere. You say, "I'd really like to have more money, *but* I just seem to work and work and never get ahead." So what did you really ask for? You really asked "to work and work and never get ahead!"

The Universe says, "Your wish is my command," and gives you the *but*. It never says *no*. It doesn't know how! It just gives you exactly what you've asked for, and you've asked for the *but*. Ouch!

Energetically, that *but* has a *characteristic feeling* or vibration that represents the overall vibration of the beliefs, assumptions or expectations that underlie it. When you ask for something that feels good as you ask, the Universe brings you that or something similar. However, thoughts that have a *but* tacked onto them seldom feel good and the fruit of those thoughts won't feel good when they show up in your experience. This gives insight into the phrase, "Be careful what you ask for," doesn't it?

The very first thing is to be aware of what's going on! If you're asking for something and not getting the results you're asking for, I can guarantee there's a big *but* in there someplace. If you're asking and that asking doesn't feel good as you ask, then what you receive is bound to make you feel exactly the same way. That's the way the system works.

So, obviously the trick is to feel good when we're asking. Right? Think about something you would like to bring into your life, but you keep getting results that are less than great. Understand that there may be silent or unconscious *buts* operating that you may not even aware of.

Think about this for a moment and just repeat the following statement. "I'd really like to have more _____ in my life." You can fill in the blank with whatever you wish to experience. As you say this, do you hear or feel a *but* in there somewhere?

Typically, this will bring a *characteristic feeling* to conscious awareness and it is this feeling we wish to address. You may wish to estimate the intensity of that feeling between zero and 10, with 10 being very intense and zero being nothing at all. The higher the intensity, the more negative energy you are holding in that *but*.

Now, mark that *characteristic feeling* with your awareness and switch on your *General Clearing* recording and release it. When you finish, repeat the statement to yourself again paying attention to how it feels as you say it to yourself. "I'd really like to have more _____ in my life." If it feels good, you can move on to your next desire, if not, just listen to the recording again.

Make a list of all of the things, circumstances and people you'd like to attract into your life. Take your time and really think about what you really want. Then, run the statements for yourself just as you did in the above example.

STILLING THE VOICE OF DOUBT WITHIN

What if every time you have a thought that says, "You'll never be able to do this," you were to immediately say to yourself, "What if I can?" and then repeat your cue word until you feel a sense of anticipation and excitement?

These voices of doubt are merely leftover programs or aspects of us whose original purpose was to keep us safe. To these voices, any action you contemplate taking that may shift you out of your comfort zone into something new and exciting is suspect, and they will often speak up to voice their concern.

For example, you suddenly have a thought about how to solve a particular problem or have an idea that could open your life to wonderful new possibilities. As you think these thoughts you grow excited. Suddenly, seemingly from out of nowhere you have a thought that says, "I'll never be able to do that." And so you put that idea aside. Henry Ford once said, "If you think you can do a thing or think you can't do a thing, you're right."

Brilliant ideas abound in this world, ideas that could change the face of the planet. But how many of those ideas are actually acted upon? Right at this moment somewhere out there, someone has an idea that could lead to a cure for cancer or a car that runs on water or a way to generate electricity that costs virtually nothing. All great advances, whether big or small, began with a simple question, "What if I can...?"

What if you can become more aware of your inner dialog and recognize those thoughts of *I can't* or *they'll never let me...* when they occur? What if these thoughts are simply leftovers from a time when you saw yourself as powerless to affect your life or the lives of others in a positive way? But what if it's not true? What if you can?

> *What if I can release that voice of doubt within me? <yes>*

> *What if I can begin the process of letting these voices go simply by being aware of them? <yes>*

> *What if every time I hear the voice of doubt and feel that distinctive feeling that always accompanies it, I mark that feeling and release it? <yes>*

> *What if whenever I hear the voice of doubt, I respond by asking, "What if I can...?" and repeat my cue word until I feel better? <yes>*

LIVING YOUR LIFE ON PURPOSE

If you've made it this far in the book and worked through some or all of the exercises, you are ready to begin living your life on purpose and allowing happiness on cue. Most people go through life not knowing or even acknowledging what it is that they really want. Most accept the suggestions of parents or peers and bow to the *reality* of earning a living and try very hard to live the same dream as everyone else. But what if that doesn't make you happy?

Every moment contains within it infinite possibilities for growth, expansion and enjoyment. If you are in a job you don't like, and can't see your way past that place, what if there was a way to bring yourself into alignment with what you really want to do, and then do it?

We are all born with talents, abilities and inclinations that if allowed expression, bring us great fulfillment and joy. Denying those abilities or inclinations places us in the position of denying who we really are inside.

Instead of fulfillment we find only the bitter taste of disappointment and open ourselves to depression, substance abuse, poor relationships or worse. A job, lifestyle or relationship that stifles your ability to express your uniqueness will always disappoint regardless of how much money you make or how perfect others may think your life to be.

Feeling dissatisfaction at the direction of your life is actually a good thing. The dissatisfaction signals you in no uncertain terms that it's time to make a fresh choice. But what do you do if you have no idea what it is you really want to do or the direction you really want to take?

So, lets begin by letting go of those feelings that prevent us from seeing ourselves and realizing our dreams in a deeper way. By now you know the drill. Just repeat the following statements and play the *General Release* recording after each one. Remember, there's no rush. If you can, view this as an adventure to an undiscovered land, and that undiscovered land is within you. So, let's begin that journey shall we?

> ➤ *When I consider the direction of my life right now, I feel... <yes>*

➤ *When I consider the dreams I have for myself, I feel... <yes>*

➤ *When I consider wanting something more for myself, I feel... <yes>*

➤ *When I consider that I may find that something more, I feel... <yes>*

➤ *When I consider letting go of the safety of my past and reaching for my dream, I feel... <yes>*

After listening to the *Clearing* recording take a breath and relax. Just check in with yourself for a moment and repeat the following statements one more time. This time however you just want to see if all the heavy feelings are gone.

➤ *When I think about the direction of my life right now, I feel... <yes>*

➤ *When I think about the dreams I have for myself, I feel... <yes>*

➤ *When I think about wanting something more for myself, I feel... <yes>*

➤ *When I think about finding that something more, I feel... <yes>*

➤ *When I consider letting go of my fear and reaching for my dream, I feel... <yes>*

If you don't feel completely peaceful and relaxed after running each statement, listen to the recording again. Once you've done this, you can use the following *What if* statements to enhance the feeling of excitement that spontaneously arises as you think about this matter. This feeling will support those new dreams and the expanded perspective that is now yours.

> ➤ *What if I allowed myself the freedom of making new choices?* <yes>
> ➤ *What if I opened myself to dreaming bigger dreams?* <yes>
> ➤ *What if I let the "hows" take care of themselves?* <yes>
> ➤ *What if I simply follow my heart and trust?* <yes>
> ➤ *What if I can actually live the life I really want?* <yes>
> ➤ *What if...?* <yes>

TO BE, TO DO AND TO HAVE

From a very early age society teaches us that to have the life we want for ourselves, to have love, money and happiness, we must first do the actions necessary that will allow us to have those things. Then we can comfortably be happy, or be secure or be loved.

For example, to be respected by your family, friends and neighbors you must work hard and take the steps necessary to earn their respect. In other words, we must do something to have something and only then can we be respected. We must *do* to *have* and then we can *be*.

But what if we've got it wrong? What if to have those things in life that make us happy we must first *be* the thing we want to be and in being that we will be inspired to take the actions necessary to have those things. We must first be to do to have.

I've designed a little exercise that will help you with both aspects of this question and it's very simple. Draw two circles, each about the size of a tennis ball, next to each other on a piece of paper. You want the circles big enough so you can write some things within each circle.

In the first circle, write down all of the things you'd rather *not have*, such as financial lack, a job you don't like or a relationship that doesn't satisfy, poor health etc. This is your starting point. In the second circle, write down what you'd *like to attract*, such as financial security, a job that has meaning or a relationship that allows you to be the person you'd truly like to be.

Pay attention to how each circle makes you feel as you read what you've written. There should be a decided difference or contrast in how the contents of those two circles make you feel. It's also likely that the contents of the second circle will seem somewhat unreal or impossible. Pay attention to both feelings.

Set the intention to bring yourself into full energetic alignment with the contents of the second circle by releasing your current alignment with the contents of the first circle. You can do this by counting down from 10 to zero while repeating your cue word between counts just as I do in the *General Clearing* recordings. In fact, if you wish, you can listen to just that part of the recording after you've filled in your circles.

Once you've finished, go back and re-read what you've written in the first circle. It's very likely that what you've written will seem distant, like someone else wrote it. And, if you look at what you've written into the second circle, those things will now seem more possible. Pay attention to how that second circle makes you feel.

Now, to complete this exercise, simply set your intention to align with the contents of the second circle and release your attachment to the contents of the first circle. Bear this intention in mind as you count down slowly from 10 to zero remembering to repeat your cue word as you do so.

Pay attention to how you feel about the second circle now. Does it feel even more possible? Just allow yourself to feel that new feeling and be aware that whatever you've placed in that circle is now on its way to you. Your job is simply to allow it and to be open to inspired action to achieve it.

CHAPTER 10

You Be the Change

"You must be the change you want

to see in the world."

—*MAHATMA GHANDI*

If you go through the exercises in this book and listen to the included recordings it won't take very long for you to become far more peaceful, poised and relaxed in situations and circumstances that formerly caused upset and drama. You, the real you will be back in charge. You'll feel happier.

Do not judge this book by it's size. Rather, judge it by the effect it has on your life, and the lives of those you come in contact with. Peace and happiness in any situation always begin with you, and the peace you carry within you will affect those around you in very powerful ways.

We live in a world that is in the midst of great change and the rate of that change appears to be accelerating. Be aware that in purchasing this book and completing the exercises, you are part of that change.

A few years ago I recall reading about an very unusual experiment carried out in 1993 that involved bringing together nearly 4,000 Transcendental Meditation practitioners from 81 countries around the world. Allow me to quote from that study[5]:

> The experiment was rigorously analyzed by a 27-member project review board composed of independent scientists and civic leaders who approved the research protocol and monitored the research process. Researchers predicted in advance that the calming influence of group meditation practice could reduce violent crime by over 20 percent in Washington, D.C., during an 8-week period in the summer of 1993.
>
> In fact, the findings later showed that the rate of violent crime decreased by 23 percent during the June 7 to July 30 experimental period. The odds of this result occurring by chance are less than 2 in 1 billion. Rigorous statistical analyses ruled out an extensive list of alternative explanations, according to John Hagelin, lead author of the study and director of the Institute of Science, Technology and Public Policy at Maharishi University of Management in Fairfield, Iowa.

---

5 See the *Washington, DC Crime Reduction Study* on the Website at http://www.tmscotland.org/world-peace.html

The predictions were lodged in advance with a panel of prominent social scientists and civic leaders, including members of the District city council and Metropolitan Police force. Statistical analysis considered the effect of weather variables, daylight, police patrolling, historical crime trends and annual patterns in the District of Columbia, as well as trends in neighboring cities.

COMMENTS ON THE STUDY

Anne Hughes, a professor of sociology and government at the University of the District of Columbia and a member of the project review board, feels that the findings of the study have significant implications for resolving inner city violence. "What we are looking at here is a new paradigm of viewing crime and violence. I would like to recommend that this new model, which is supported by a number of exhaustive and very carefully controlled studies, be seriously considered, and that we think about ways that it might be implemented in the inner city."

David Edwards, another member of the project review board, and professor of government at the University of Texas at Austin, believes this research and the theory behind it deserve the most serious consideration. "I think the claim can be plausibly made that the potential impact of this research exceeds that of any other ongoing social or psychologi-

cal research program. It has survived a broader ar-
ray of statistical tests than most research in the field
of conflict resolution. This work and the theory that
informs it deserve the most serious consideration by
academics and policy makers alike.

I mentioned earlier in this book that using ZPoint leads you into a deep meditative state as you practice it. From an energy perspective, it also significantly raises your vibration or overall energy signature. It is my belief that as more and more people use energy practices in general and ZPoint in particular, this will have an increasing impact on world peace.

I believe this simply because it's much quicker and easier to reach that deep meditative state with ZPoint, especially for those who don't have the time or the inclination to practice traditional meditation.

At the end of my correspondence. It reads, "Peace always begins with me!" These are not just words, they are a statement of fact. No matter what situation I find myself in, peace and happiness always begins with me.

When I walk into a room, no matter what's going on, I am peaceful and that peace extends like a bubble around me. When I speak to people or even just sit near them, they become more peaceful too, often remarkably so.

I am not the only person who has this effect on people. There are many long time ZPoint Process users who have noticed this phenomenon as well. It is important to understand that it is not our personalities affecting people in this way. It is the peace we carry inside us that does this.

When you are peaceful inside, that peace can be felt by everyone you come into contact with just as the opposite is true. It is a palpable presence that you carry within you and that presence reaches out to others and affects them as well.

It has long been known and accepted that "as it is within you, so shall it be outside of you." If you are filled with upset and anger or resentment, you will attract exactly those situations, circumstances and relationships that mirror that upset. Your life on the outside will be filled with a turmoil that merely reflects the turmoil already present within you.

If you feel abused, you will notice only those experiencing similar abuse. If you are angry, you will constantly meet that anger in relationships or the circumstances and situations that trigger it. As it is within you, so shall it be outside of you.

The purpose of learning and doing the ZPoint Process is to help you stop the drama and the upset. Its purpose is to give you a simple way to let all of that go and find inner peace and happiness.

Many people today are concerned with world peace or outer peace. They look at the world and see only the violence, the mistrust, the anger and the resentment. They feel powerless to do anything about the current situation and in their powerlessness feel isolated and alone.

To feel better about themselves, they join organizations believing that in working with others, in promoting the idea of world peace this will cause others to change. In asking those people to become peaceful the world will become more peaceful as a result.

I am here to tell you that this approach *will not* work. We cannot change the world by trying to change others. We can *only change ourselves.* If this approach did work, we would be experiencing a far more peaceful world right now.

Mahatma Ghandi said it best, "Be the change you want to see in the world." This means that if you want a peaceful world, you must first become peaceful within yourself. Peace always begins with you and spreads outward. To say to another, "lay down your arms and find peace," without first feeling that peace within you, is a complete waste of effort. You are saying, "Do as I say, not as I do." These are merely empty words as there is no power of truth behind them.

When you speak words of peace and inside secretly think thoughts of anger or resentment, you perpetrate the very conditions you seek to change. First, become peaceful within yourself and then your words and your very presence will have the power to change lives. Peace and happiness always begin with you.

If you are truly committed to world peace, find that peace within yourself first. Over a very short period of time you'll notice yourself becoming much more peaceful and relaxed about life, and this is a gift beyond measure.

All parts of your life will change for the better. You will be happier and you will see that happiness reflected in the faces around you. Remember, as within, so without. And the greatest part is, you don't need to say a word. You become that peace personified.

Practice the ZPoint Process every day and become more and more peaceful within yourself. You will very quickly see the results of the peace you carry as it powerfully affects your relationships and everything you touch. Be the change you want to see in the world. Be at peace with the world and the world will smile back at you.

You are making a difference to the world and to yourself each time you use the ZPoint Process and become happier within yourself. We are all connected. When you release difficult feelings and grow happier within your own life, you affect those around you in very positive ways.

Like me, you'll notice yourself smiling at strangers and have them smile back at you. You'll see people treating you with genuine respect and consideration, as you extend those same considerations to all you meet. Be the change you want to see in the world. Peace does indeed begin with you and so does *allowing happiness on cue.*

ZPointforPeace.com

CHAPTER 11

Next Step... ZPoint Process Resources

"Few things are impossible

to diligence and skill."

—*SAMUEL JOHNSON*

The purpose of this book has been to introduce you to the ZPoint Process. It's a quick start or kickstart. The more you do the ZPoint Process, the more adept you'll be at it.

Happiness is a natural state of being. You can use the ZPoint process in every area of your life to clear away anything that might make you feel unhappy.

To further your abilities with the ZPoint Process, please visit our Website at *ZPointforPeace.com*. Here you'll find programs for specific issues such as eliminating anger, stress, worry and fear.

You can also find certified ZPoint Practitioners you can work with in various countries around the world. You don't have to work with a practitioner in person. Most ZPoint Practitioners can consult with you very effectively over the phone.

There' are also details on live seminars, Webinars and coaching programs. If you're interested in becoming a certified ZPoint Practitioner, you can take one of the trainings offered on a regular basis. It's all at:

ZPointforPeace.com

CHAPTER 12

ZPoint Process Stories

"The critical ingredient is getting

off your butt and doing something.

It's as simple as that. Not tomorrow.

Not next week. But today.

—*ROBERT BROWNING*

Now that you have a simple powerful tool to bring more happiness on cue to your life, what's next? Get into the positive habit of doing the ZPoint Process on a regular basis to clear away the things that are behind you feeling unhappy.

On the following pages, you'll find stories from people like you who have discovered the ZPoint Process and used it to create positive results to relieve all kinds of issues. Start today. Right now. One step is all it takes. The sooner you do, the sooner you'll feel a difference.

RELEASING PAINFUL 55 YEAR OLD MEMORIES

It's taken me some time to get to this but here are the details. I'm 62 years old and have applied many healing and releasing processes to a specific group of past memories. Regardless of how big the insights or how determined I have been to rid myself of the negative impact of those memories, I had not budged the energy one bit until I used the ZPoint Process to guide me through a period of time in my childhood.

I went through the entire process and immediately afterward noticed that I no longer felt any energy around the memories. It's been two weeks and I still haven't felt any energy around those memories. I can actually even imagine that I might someday forget about them entirely. Again, thank you for sharing this process. It is so good to be free of the pain that emanated from those 55 year old memories.

—Joyce

Releasing Difficult Feelings in a Marriage

After going through the relationship process, I am feeling much more compassionate towards my husband. The preparation for our home remodeling has been very stressful for him. He's been very short tempered and anxious as we packed and loaded the contents of the first floor of the house into a pod, and made lots of decisions about the project.

I have been able to see him as someone who is struggling with all this change, chaos, expense and anxiety over the project. He is also feeling some anxiety about how I am changing. He has fears about being left behind. I see him as vulnerable instead of my usual thoughts of how selfish, rude and obnoxious he is.

The other day he said something. I don't even remember what he said, but I had a flash of tremendous anger, and then an immediate thought of compassion and forgiveness. This is quite a change, I used to dwell on things like this for days, replaying over and over in my mind how he "did me wrong," and how I deserve better, etc.

It's much easier for me to just let stuff go now. His sister and her family were here for 10 days. I was expecting to be very fed up by the end, but I really enjoyed myself and was able to let a lot of minor annoyances just slide. If things were not going the way I preferred, I was easily able to just let it go.

I'm loving the ZPoint Process! It's been very helpful. I did the "what if" stuff this morning. "What if all the packing up goes easily and is actually fun?" "What if it's easy for me to get rid of stuff I no longer need?" Tonight I heard myself tell someone that the remodeling was going much easier than I expected.

—Sandra

RELEASING A BURDEN OF SHAME

This Christmas is very different for me. I've lost weight. I do not stress, and my innermost fears of failure and non-worthiness have evaporated. It all started with my wife telling me about The ZPoint Process that she found on the Internet. I was a bit reluctant trying something new again, yet I did. After doing the setup and the body image script, I yawned a lot.

I was tired and didn't feel much change. The next morning I woke up with a very different feeling in my body, like something was missing. Slowly I realized that a burden of shame coming from my childhood was gone. Not to say I do not have problems, but this deep rooted feeling is finito, gone, erased like a weight that suddenly disappeared!

I do not understand this intellectually, but I do love the results, this new feeling of lightness. Since then, I have had done ZPoint all the time, experiencing waves of clear seeing and also in between some fear of change, even when it's to the better. I just keep persistently using even more ZPoint on it.

It's now a habit that every time a distressing thought creeps up on me, I quickly change these patterns. I also use EFT but have the experience that it works better with my clients than when I do it for myself.

I also have used Grant's idea of a symbol for healing with two clients suffering from PTSD, helping them to get a full night's sleep. (This was a combination of EFT and using the ZPoint statements). I think the calm inner peace feeling I'm experiencing in my life will enable me to get even more positive abundance and inner peace.

I hope this can encourage even more people to use The ZPoint Process. I also think an important part of the gift of ZPoint is that it's rooted in a positive approach to change and not a fear based healing method. The ZPoint Process is extremely powerful. Twenty years of therapy with mixed results and a deep rooted beliefs disappeared. This new me with more genuine feelings and more creativity emerged beautifully within a very short time.

I feel as if the past is the past and the future is the future. My part of is just to be in the in between one breath a time, here and now. This is a very empowering experience. Thanks, I did not know this was possible in this lifetime.

—Chris

PROFOUND, EFFORTLESS AND PAINLESS

My wife and I have tried many forms of inner healing over the years and I can honestly say that no other modality has given such a good result as the ZPoint Process. Not only are the results profound, they are effortless and painless to achieve as well. I wouldn't have believed that inner work can be so easy to do as this.

This morning when I woke up, and even now as I write this after attending to the day's business, I still have the same warm, fuzzy ball of pure white energy in my solar plexus. The inner calmness that I feel is something that I cannot recall ever having in my conscious memory.

While I am sure that events and circumstances will cause this to fade, I know that listening to the audios I have downloaded will bring me back to this incredible inner peace that I have searched for all my life. Thank you again for sharing such an incredible tool and be reassured that we will do our utmost to help others to receive this gift too.

—Charles

Achieve My Potential

I have been on an exhausting search for a decade to uncover a process or healing technique that would help me heal and break the pattern of self-destruction that has been the story of my life after a particularly traumatic event.

I've subsequently tried Reiki, Kinesiology, the Horstmann Technique and many other forms of healing over the past decade but none have been so transformative, all encompassing or profoundly healing as my experience of the ZPoint Process. So please accept a humble thank you from me.

Issues of safety, self-esteem, my blocks to happiness, inner peace and love were all resolved today. I would like to see how it will now positively impact my future. I am convinced that this experience will be life changing and far reaching.

This has been the best present I have ever given myself, and I know that it will help me to live in and appreciate the present for the gift that it is and to let go of my traumatic past and all the emotional baggage that's been the result of the pain and the fear I've been carrying with me. No more.

So thank you! I feel at peace and free to follow my bliss, with the self belief that I can and will achieve my potential and let my true self (spirit) shine! My future is filled with possibilities and free of the shackles of the past. Wow!

—Tracey

Regained Vision

I have a severe astigmatism and am extremely near-sighted. I remembered that my vision got significantly worse almost overnight, but I had a hard time recalling exactly when that was. I do remember that my opthamologist commented on how unusual it was for someone's vision to get that much worse so quickly, particularly without any obvious medical reasons for it.

I decided to do some detective work and determine exactly when this happened and compare it to what had been going on in my life at the time. I got my records from my doctor and determined that it occurred sometime in the late spring of 1989. This was the major revelation for me.

In the spring of that year, while I was in graduate school in Colorado, I was pulled over by what was apparently an unmarked police car, only to discover it was not the police, but someone masquerading as the police. I was beaten and violently raped. I was called in to a police line-up after a suspect was apprehended. Unfortunately, I was unable to pick someone out of the line-up, since it was nighttime when the incident occurred, and I did not get a good look at him. Everything happened so fast, and I was unconscious for a time afterwards. I felt so horrible that I could not make the ID and that this man might go free, all because I could not remember enough about what he looked like. Not long after that, my vision went from 20/200 to 20/600 and my astigmatism developed. Aha!

I used a lot of suggestions about clearing statements and ETT, and then just let my mind go wild. I honestly can't even remember most of the statements as they just flowed from me. I erased so much pain and guilt surrounding this incident and its likely correlation to my vision problems.

I actually fell asleep while doing this and didn't wake up until the next morning. My first thought was, "Darn it I fell asleep with my contact lenses on," but then I remembered I had removed them prior to starting my clearing statements.

I could see and I wasn't wearing my contacts. Normally, I would have to fumble around with my hands to find my glasses on the night stand, since I can't even see that far to find them. I could see the clock clear across the room!

This is the most amazing and powerful thing that has ever happened to me. I saw my opthamologist yesterday afternoon and he was completely at a loss for words.

—Cathy

SOMETHING'S WORKING FOR ME

I must admit that while I don't understand what this process is doing for me, it is definitely doing something. My mind is so much calmer and more settled.

I'm not as hard on myself. I'm forgiving myself easily and moving on from the little mistakes that occur in a day, like not expecting myself to be perfect and beating myself up when I'm not. What makes all this more remarkable is that I'm an overly busy single mom of three young girls who was laid off three weeks ago, with nothing in the bank and no cash in my pocket.

I've had a very sick four year old child with me 100% of the day since her daycare ended and new daycare doesn't start for another week. I've been accepting the flow of my days and the limitations that are keeping me from full out job hunting in my typical high performance, anxious, manic way. I'm not worrying nearly as much about money and bills, but I am manifesting bit-by-bit what we truly need through faith and confidence in the Universe and the process. It's wonderful.

—Kimberly

Two Instances of Physical Trauma

I've had the opportunity in the past two weeks to apply ETT (ZPoint's *Erase the Tape* Method) to two occurrences of physical trauma with amazing results. The first time occurred this last Friday evening. I decided it was time to trim a candle that had burned down in the center. With a big butcher knife in hand, I set about my task. All was going well until the knife slipped and punctured my left hand in the web between the thumb and index finger. Blood was spurting everywhere!

I grabbed a piece of ice and a paper towel and began focusing on replaying the series of events just until the knife punctured my hand. Then I began counting down from 10 to zero while silently repeating my cue word. I then counted from zero to 10, repeating my cue word and running the images of the event in my mind.

The pain decreased substantially, and I was able to uneventfully get to the emergency room for stitches. Because of the location of the cut, the doctor could not numb the entire area so once again that cue word was repeated as the sutures were being placed. The hospital staff was surprised that I didn't need anything for pain.

The second event was a couple of weeks ago when I opened my car door. The glass was rolled up and in my haste to get to work I opened the door very quickly and slammed the glass into my forehead. I got into the car and started running the events that led up to me hitting my head with the door and then stopped. I also began counting down from 10 and by the time I got to four, the pain and swelling were gone.

I'm usually a non-klutzy person. Perhaps these two events were just to demonstrate to me, again, how powerful ZPoint is. Whew, what do folks do without ETT, ZPoint and cue words?

—Martha

Better Relationship with My Father

I have come a long way in a short time using this amazing process. Sometimes you don't even realize you have made huge strides forward until you find yourself in a situation and become aware that you are reacting differently.

I had a big falling out with my father three years ago. Since then, I have refused to visit my parents' home and tried to avoid getting him on the phone when I call my mother. He was ill recently, and I visited him in the hospital. When he got out, I stayed at their home for five or six days without arguing. That would have been a complete impossibility prior to using ZPoint.

I had used EFT on my issues with my dad, but he still irritated me, and I still argued with him. It wasn't until I came home that I became aware that we actually had a very enjoyable time and although we will probably never understand each other, we didn't fight! Your audios have reminded me to remain aware of where I am behaving differently even if it is very subtle, and not to forget to do my ZPoint Process daily.

—Barbara

Releasing Long Standing Anxiety

I just wanted to say how great I think the ZPoint Process is. I have tried many other energy techniques and they are all good but ZPoint really resonates with me.

I have used the ZPoint Process for anxiety and daily alignment regularly the last couple of weeks. I've been experiencing wonderful changes in my life and how I react to certain situations. Just listening to the audios completely relaxes me, which is something I have a hard time doing. Plus, abundance seems to be coming into all areas of my life!

I had been doing the process for a couple of months and making some progress but nothing big until I focused on the anxiety. I guess persistence pays off.

—Amanda

CHANGED MY LIFE

First of all, if anyone thinks the ZPoint Process doesn't work, they're just wrong, wrong, wrong. Grant Connolly said that three weeks after his workshop, we wouldn't be able to recognize our lives. Well, it'll be three weeks this coming Tuesday and I already don't recognize my life.

Procrastination? Gone. Not an issue anymore. Weight loss? Try 20 pounds in the last month. I know that's fast, but I swear I'm eating when I'm hungry. I just don't want bread, sugar, pasta, or heavy food. I only eat when I'm hungry, and I fill up really fast. My biggest problem is that my pants are falling right off, and I have to keep buying smaller sizes.

I also stated my intention for a loving relationship. That's been a bit weird. At first, my husband started responding somewhat lovingly to me. Generally he just treats me like I'm invisible, or a servant. That stopped finally and he went back to his old ways. Oh, well. But then, these men I was acquainted with basically came out of the woodwork, expressing an attraction for me. Four of them. Yes, four of them.

Now, I'm not taking any of them up on their offers because I'm married. Maybe not happily so, but still married. Still, the offers were there. And my circle of friends just keeps growing and growing. I feel like I've got my mojo back. So maybe I don't have that loving relationship, but I'm surrounded by love, and that's just about as good. I'm presently being very careful what I ask for.

This method is so amazing. I'm so happy. My boss has been telling the shareholders how happy he is with my work. What else can I say? Wow!

—Crystal

Releasing Fear

I love the way that *A Course In Miracles* distills feelings down to two things. It makes it really easy for me to know where I'm at—either love or fear. All feelings distill down to one or the other.

Hatred, anger, envy, jealousy, irritation, depression, sadness, worry, greed, etc. are all expressions of fear. All expressions of fear can be healed with love. The ZPoint Process is helping to heal all of my expressions of fear, and I feel happier, more peaceful, and more loving.

My life is in a very precarious position financially. In the past, I'd have been sick with worry and fear—terror, more likely. I feel calm, peaceful and relaxed, knowing that all is well and I am just fine. And, things are getting better.

I think that everything that hurts is just something to learn about ourselves. When I bump up against things that hurt now, instead of running and hiding, it is much easier to sit still, look and clear it.

It's not necessary to weld myself to trouble. Fear and all attendant troubles used to be how I defined myself. If I couldn't complain, I had nothing to say to people and had no way to know who I was.

I've been telling everyone who will listen how awesome the ZPoint Process is. Many of the changes are so very subtle that I don't even realize them until I'm in a situation that would normally have produced some amount of discomfort, and, there is none. It's much easier to remember to relax, breathe and say my cue word.

In the past, if someone had said or done something that I felt hurt, angry or upset about, I'd keep poking at it to keep the hurt alive, to remember so that I wouldn't do something like that again. Of course, that didn't work. It just kept me depressed, angry and upset.

Not any longer. I feel more peaceful in formerly stressful situations. I'm calmer and happier more of the time. When something is upsetting, I don't stay in the upset, mostly because I can't remember what the upset was.

I feel more confident and relaxed. I switched gears career wise from playing in a classroom to business meetings and networking groups. I was depressed for the better part of a year because I felt so out of place and very uncomfortable until the ZPoint Process.

I'm focused on being happy and having fun. Business meetings and groups are cake and pie now. After beginning to use the ZPoint Process, a thought kept running through my head—elegance, grace and ease.

I've completely renounced struggle and effort. I'm not always completely successful at it. I still pick up struggle sometimes, yet I don't hang onto it. I'm really aware that I am and always have been a very happy person who learned to be very unhappy.

I laugh and play more. I'm finally almost completely comfortable in my own skin. There isn't a single area of my life that I can't or don't use the process and there isn't a single area of my life that hasn't changed for the better.

—Karen

Releasing Anger

Yesterday I was working with a client who has a violent, volatile temper. Whenever he gets irritated, annoyed, or upset, he swears a blue streak. He has been using the ZPoint Process for a week or so and has caught on fast, using his cue word "relax" at every opportunity. But when he gets mad, he gets sidetracked, and it's an effort for him to switch mental gears and remember to use his cue word.

So we did an experiment by instructing his subconscious mind that whenever he thought or said any of the curse words in his vocabulary—he listed seven words that he uses most often—his subconscious mind would recognize the word as a cue word and immediately start clearing out everything pertaining to the issue at hand.

It worked immediately and very well. He reported that every time he started to lose his temper, got upset, muttered under his breath, thought a curse word, or swore out loud, his energy shifted quickly away from the problem. He said it was kind of scary. Anger is such a well-established habit with him, it felt weird to immediately lose track of what he was upset about. His anger just evaporated!

—CJ

About the Author

Yes, you can change your life. Grant Connolly is living proof. He had a very unhappy childhood, got bullied, dropped out of high school, and felt like a failure for many years. No more.

Today, his life is rich, full and deeply satisfying. In short, he's having the best time of his life. After going back to school in his early thirties to study technology—computers and communications—he followed his passion and worked with computers for a number of years. Fascinated with how the subconscious mind works, Grant became a certified hypnotist.

Using his greatest abilities—following his intuition and synthesizing everything he's learned—he developed a simple, powerful process to transform his life by clearing away all the things that made him feel unhappy. He says that when we clear all of the things that we are not, underneath we'll find the person we've always wanted to be.

In addition to being an author, Grant is a coach and trainer, teaching his process online and at live seminars around the world. Grant was born and raised in Peterborough, Ontario, Canada. He still calls it home, (except when it's cold outside!) :-)

www.ingramcontent.com/pod-product-compliance
Lightning Source LLC
Chambersburg PA
CBHW032016090426

42741CB00006B/621